Hydrangeas

*H*YDRANGEAS

DARIA PRICE BOWMAN

FRIEDMAN/FAIRFAX
P U B L I S H E R S

A FRIEDMAN/FAIRFAX BOOK

© 2000, 1999 by Michael Friedman Publishing Group, Inc.

Library of Congress Cataloging-in-Publication Data available upon request.

ISBN 1-56799-737-6

Editor: Susan Lauzau
Art Director: Jeff Batzli
Designer: Andrea Karman
Photography Editor: Amy Talluto
Production Manager: Camille Lee

Color separations by Colourscan Overseas Co Pte Ltd.
Printed in Hong Kong by Midas Printing Limited

3 5 7 9 10 8 6 4 2

For bulk purchases and special sales, please contact:
Friedman/Fairfax Publishers
Attention: Sales Department
15 West 26th Street
New York, New York 10010
212/685-6610   FAX 212/685-1307

Dedication and Acknowledgments

For Patricia McKearn, my friend, my partner, and my inspiration.

Special thanks go to Section Gardener Ed Broadbent of Longwood Gardens and to Steve Cooper, Manager of Imperatore Nurseries, for sharing their expertise.

Introduction

 think I first noticed hydrangeas when I was about thirteen years old. I remember seeing them as I rode my bike in the neighborhood of our summer home in Woods Hole, Massachusetts. There they were, a big tumble of vivid blue blooms, made all the more vibrant against the weathered gray of an old house.

Those venerable hydrangeas are still there—just as vivid, and, if anything, even more beautiful. Perhaps my thirteen-year-old will notice them this summer as she rides her bike along the same street.

In my own tiny garden, a massive blue lacecap, started from a rooted cutting bought from another Cape Cod gardener a dozen years ago, resides in our side garden under the protective branches of a katsura tree. Three smaller lacecaps live across the brick path awaiting transplant to other parts of the garden. When these plants are in bloom, passersby will often stop and stare at their breathtaking beauty.

A few years ago, when I launched a landscape design business with a dear friend, I was struck by the number of clients who, though they had very few requests for specific plants, wanted to include hydrangeas in their gardens. One woman asked for "a big hydrangea tree like the one my grandmother had." She was referring to the beautiful and blowzy PeeGee hydrangea that does indeed

Opposite: *Hydrangea macrophylla*

seem grandmotherly in its old-fashioned loveliness. Another client was nostalgic for her beloved Nantucket home, so in designing her New Jersey garden, my partner and I tucked a few hydrangeas in shades of pink and blue into the small urban space.

I am always happy to oblige our landscape customers' desires for hydrangeas, for I know that these plants will perform admirably, even with the benign neglect that may befall them. And somehow, with every hydrangea we plant, we have the small though joyful satisfaction of having made a beautiful addition to our surroundings.

In the pages that follow, you will find spectacular photographs of many types of hydrangeas in gardens on both sides of the Atlantic. There are suggestions for using hydrangeas in the landscape, ideas for plants that make good companions

Above: The petals of this unnamed Japanese species are delicately wrought.

for these blowzy shrubs, and details on how to dry the beautiful blooms for indoor enjoyment. And you will learn how each member of this outstanding group of plants differs from its cousins, as well as the secrets of cultivating and caring for them.

For some readers, the information may be useful. For others, the photos may evoke nostalgic and pleasant thoughts. My hope is that all who read these pages will find a new appreciation for one of our most treasured garden plants.

Daria Price Bowman
New Hope, Pennsylvania

Above: Intense blue florets add color to the summer garden.

Through the Years

Though relatively new to garden cultivation, at least compared with plants like roses or carnations, the hydrangea is very, very old. Hydrangeas originally lived in the temperate forests of the northern hemisphere covering what we know today as Manchuria, Greenland, and Alaska as early as 65 million years ago. Paleontologists have found hydrangea fossils in the northwest region of North America, as well as in China, Japan, and Korea.

It was in the eighteenth century, when European and particularly English plant collectors searched the globe for exotic new plants, that hydrangeas first began to appear in garden literature. According to garden historian Alice M. Coats, the first hydrangea introduced in England was *Hydrangea arborescens* (wild hydrangea), purchased in 1736 by Peter Collinson, a plant collector, perhaps from the American horticulturist John Bartram. This native plant was known to Americans, though it may not have been cultivated.

Another American native, the oak-leaf hydrangea (*Hydrangea quercifolia*), was discovered by John Bartram in the last quarter of the eighteenth century. He sold specimens to an English collector around 1805. In the 1860s, *H. arborescens grandiflora* (commonly called snowhill hydrangea) was found in the wild, either in Pennsylvania or Ohio, depending on which expert one reads, and in 1907 it was recognized with an Award of Merit by the Royal Horticultural Society.

Opposite: The lush blooms of hydrangeas have proved irresistible for centuries.

Old–Fashioned Loveliness

The mophead varieties of hydrangea were especially favored during the Victorian era, when excess in design—whether of houses, furniture, clothing, or in the garden—was de rigeur. The huge, blowzy fullness of hydrangea blooms seemed created just for the over-the-top frilliness of that time.

Later, hydrangeas fell out of favor, for the very reasons they were beloved by earlier generations. Now, as cottage garden styling and the richness of old-fashioned mixed borders have returned with vigor to garden design, hydrangeas have once again found themselves utterly desirable.

Above: *Hydrangea macrophylla*   Opposite: *H. macrophylla hortensis*

What's In a Name?

One bit of confusing hydrangea history focuses on the wonderful mophead types and how their other commonly used name, hortensia, came about. Some horticulture folklorists believe that a French botanist named de Jussieu gave the shrubs that name in 1789. Alice M. Coats, an Englishwoman whose book *Garden Shrubs and their Histories* was published in 1963, claimed differently.

Hydrangea macrophylla

According to Ms. Coats:

...the astronomer Guillaume Joseph Hyacinthe

Jean-Baptiste Lengentil de la Galaisiere, who brought

some (hydrangea) plants from the East Indies...in 1771,

suggested that it should be called Leautia, after Mme.

Lepaute, wife of a celebrated clockmaker and herself an

astronomer of merit. The French botanist Commerson,

preferred however to give it the name of Hortensia; not

after Queen Hortense, the daughter of the Empress

Josephine, but after Mlle. Hortense de Nassau, daughter

of the Prince of Nassau, a distinguished botanist.

Further confusing the matter, another botanist, J. E. Smith, named a hydrangea found in China in 1792 *Hydrangea hortensis*, which later came to be called *Hydrangea hortensia*. Today we call the same plant *Hydrangea macrophylla*, though to this day, many people continue to refer to mophead hydrangeas as hortensias.

Hydrangea Lore

Unlike many plants cultivated by the ancients, including the rose, bay tree, ivy, and myrtle, hydrangeas are relative newcomers to the West. While legends and lore surrounding hydrangeas have existed for centuries in Japan and China, European stories are a mere two hundred years old.

Hydrangea experts Toni Lawson-Hall and Brian Rothera in their research found a number of obscure uses for hydrangea plants:

Hanna Matsuri is Japan's national Flower Festival held every year on April 8. During the festivities, it is traditional to pour a special "celestial" tea over a statue of Buddha. The tea is made from hydrangea leaves.

In Japan the leaves of some native hydrangeas were used to make a natural sweetener.

It is traditional among a small group of people from Hokkaido, in northern Japan, to make smoking pipes from the wood of H*ydrangea paniculata.*

The Cherokee Indians used roots of H. *arborescens for medicinal purposes, including the treatment of kidney stones.*

The Chinese used dried hydrangea flowers to treat heat stroke and malaria.

In Derbyshire, wells are decorated with "pictures" created from thousands of hydrangea sepals in a tradition dating back to ancient times.

Cicely Mary Barker's enchanting book of the 1920s, The Meaning of Flowers, recounts that hydrangeas signify a boaster because the showy flowers are never followed by fruit.

Family Album

ydrangeas belong to a large and distinguished family. But alas, due to unresolved arguments in plant nomenclature, the family is known by some as Saxifragaceae and by others as Hydrangeaceae. There are as many as eight genera and twelve hundred species within the family, which includes some of the garden's most beloved flowering shrubs and perennials.

Close relatives of hydrangeas include the Rocky Mountain native called cliff jamesia and the *Jamesia americana*, which is relatively unknown outside botanical circles. *J. americana* is a deciduous, hardy shrub that produces fragrant, star-shaped, white flowers in late spring.

A far more famous cousin is the exquisitely scented mock orange (*Philadelphus* spp.), which has graced North American gardens for generations and is equally popular in English country gardens.

The beautiful American native, *Itea virginiana*, or summersweet, known for its lovely scent and vibrant autumn foliage, is another famous hydrangea cousin. Astilbe, coralbells, and the dainty *Tiarella*, or foam flower, are also among the hydrangea's illustrious relatives.

Opposite: *Hydrangea aspera*

Glorious Flowers

The flower of the hydrangea is produced in a variety of shapes, including the spectacular mopheads, the more subtle but still exquisite lacecaps, and the elegantly attenuated conical forms. Flower shapes are one of the ways we can identify the genus and the species, and, in some cases, the variety of hydrangea we are observing.

But in order to truly understand hydrangeas, one must learn a few important horticultural terms that help to define the different parts of the flowers. Most of the terms are scientific, to be sure. However, by committing just a few words to memory, we can then grasp the essential differences that make hydrangeas unique.

The basic vocabulary of hydrangea blooms includes:

Corymb—The flat-topped or curved cluster of flowers that forms the flower head of the hydrangea. These flower clusters grow from different parts of the main stem.

Inflorescence—The part of the plant that produces flowers. A corymb is a type of inflorescence.

Sepal—The outer part of the flower that, on hydrangeas, appears as a flower petal.

Pedicel—The tiny stalk that supports a single flower in the flower head.

Petal—The individual inner part of a flower, often colorful and showy.

Sterile Flower—What we perceive as the decorative flowers of hydrangea are in fact enlarged sepals. The sepals are either distributed around the margin of the corymb or are distributed throughout the panicle. Most likely, these sterile flowers are intended to attract insects to the plant. Mophead, or hortensia, hydrangea flowers are composed almost entirely of sterile flowers made up of differing numbers of sepals.

Fertile Flower—The fertile flower is, scientifically speaking, the actual flower. These true flowers are grouped together in the center of the corymb, or may be distributed throughout the inflorescence. In some species, fertile flowers make up the entire "flower" head. Fertile flowers supply insects with nectar and are fertilized in the process. Lacecap hydrangeas are most often composed of a group of delicate fertile flowers surrounded by the showier sterile flowers.

Above: Mopheads are composed mainly of sepals rather than true flowers.   Overleaf: Buds on a hydrangea bloom.

Leafy Greens

e do most often grow hydrangeas for their exquisite bloom. But, in truth, their leaves are often very beautiful, though in a more subtle manner than the flowers. Some hydrangea varieties have quite distinct and notable foliage, and while we might not select these cultivars solely on the merit of the leaves, they add considerably to the plants' worth.

The leaves of hydrangeas range in shape from the aptly named oak-leaf forms to the typical elongated egg shape, broader at the base than the top, and the elliptic form, which is wide at the middle and elongated at the top and bottom. Hydrangea leaves are often highly textured, and many have lovely and distinctive toothed or serrated edges.

Any discussion of hydrangea foliage must focus on the exceptional oak-leaf varieties—so unusual as to have the varietal name reflective of that most distinguishing feature. With leaves shaped much like those of oak trees, *Hydrangea quercifolia* (*Quercus* being the genus of the venerable oak) is grown for those leaves nearly as much as it is for the outstanding flower. The coarse leaves have an unusual rough texture that has been described as "quilted." And few hydrangea leaves color so spectacularly as do these—in autumn they are brilliant in shades of red, purple, burgundy, and dark green.

Hydrangea paniculata 'Praecox' produces another arresting leaf color—the young new leaves arrive in vibrant yellow tones that mature to a medium green. This yellow leaf is especially striking against a dark evergreen screen. In addition, many of the big-leaf and wild hydrangeas produce vivid red tones in their autumn foliage.

Above: Hydrangea foliage   Overleaf: Lacecap and mophead hydrangeas

Growing Hydrangeas

As extraordinarily beautiful as they are, hydrangeas are remarkably simple to grow, requiring little more than a good, rich soil and adequate moisture with good drainage. Many varieties, especially the oak-leaf types (*Hydrangea quercifolia*) require a bit of protection from the sun. Hydrangeas of all types seem to resent windy conditions.

In general, hydrangeas thrive in moderate climates, Zone 4 to Zone 7 or 8. A few, notably the wild hydrangea (*Hydrangea arborescens*) and *Hydrangea paniculata*, will do perfectly well in the harsher temperatures of Zone 3. The big-leaf types (*Hydrangea macrophylla*) are less hardy, preferring to live in Zone 6 or further south.

Though generally resistant to diseases and pests, hydrangeas planted in inappropriate situations, those stressed by drought, extreme heat, or wind, or plants that have been injured may be subject to attack. But experienced gardeners rarely complain about persistent difficulties. To ensure adequately rich soil, add generous quantities of well-rotted manure and compost either to the planting hole before installation, or as a top dressing for an existing planting. A nice thick layer of mulch will help the soil retain moisture. And of course, thorough garden cleanup is a must.

Opposite: Healthy hydrangeas require little commitment from the gardener.

Big-Leaf Hydrangea

It seems odd that big-leaf hydrangea (*Hydrangea macrophylla*) is named for its foliage, which though pretty enough, cannot claim the spectacular qualities of its flowers.

These are the "typical" hydrangeas, the ones grown in pots for the florists' trade, and the ones that come most to mind when hydrangeas are the subject at hand. Big-leaf hydrangea is most often described in terms of its flowers, which are of two types—there are the hemispherical mopheads (also known as hortensias) and the flatter lacecaps.

Often appearing as great round balls, the extravagant mophead blooms are composed of many sterile flowers constructed of four or five sepals. The colors of these voluptuous blooms range from vivid blues and purple-reds to mauve, pink, rose, and white.

Lacecaps, with their center of quiet flowers, ringed with a whorl of showier blooms, have a more subtle appeal. In fact, many gardeners prefer the ethereal beauty of lacecaps to the lavish display of their more ostentatious cousins.

Dozens, if not scores, of cultivars are sold by garden centers and nurseries throughout Europe and the United States, though many varieties are available only from highly specialized sources.

Opposite: *Hydrangea macrophylla* var. *macrophylla*   Overleaf: *H. macrophylla* 'Red Rock'

Oak-Leaf Hydrangea

Tall and elegantly sprawling, the oak-leaf hydrangea (*Hydrangea quercifolia*) is a lovely native American plant that now makes its home on both sides of the Atlantic.

The oak-leaf hydrangea will climb up to six feet (1.8m), and is often trained gently up a wall. It grows happily in shady spots and is hardy as far north as Zone 5, though it will also tolerate the warmth of Zone 9. In the autumn, its large, coarse, oak-leaf-shaped leaves change from their summer cloak of dark green to a stunning array of wine reds and purples.

An especially beautiful cultivar called 'Snow Queen' earned her royal name with large creamy flower cones that stand straight up with a regal bearing. As the flowers mature, they take on a rosy beige glow that persists well into autumn.

A younger relative is 'Snowflake', which has massive flower cones—with layers of sepals on each floret. It is especially striking late in the season as the sepals change color from palest green to cream to pink to rose and finally beige, with all those colors appearing in unison.

Above: *Hydrangea quercifolia* in bloom
Opposite: *H. quercifolia* and *H. macrophylla*
Overleaf: Autumn leaves of *H. quercifolia*

Climbing Hydrangea

here are some gardeners who think there is no more satisfactory vine than the climbing hydrangea. And though it appears occasionally in nursery catalogs and from time to time in small displays at garden centers, *Hydrangea anomala* ssp. *petiolaris* (or in some references called simply *Hydrangea petiolaris*) remains a relative unknown in the North American landscape. Though more often seen in England, even among experienced gardeners this extraordinary woody vine is far from common.

And yet, with its attractive leathery leaves, showy blooms, reddish brown woody branches, and willingness to grow in shady places, the climbing hydrangea should be high on gardeners' lists of "must haves." One of the reasons, perhaps, that this hydrangea cousin is rarely included in garden plans is that it is still somewhat difficult to find. Because growers respond to market trends, if few gardeners are asking for it, few climbing hyrangeas will be grown...an unfortunate cycle.

Another reason for its scarcity is that some gardeners find raising a climbing hydrangea to be a bit of a challenge. These extraordinarily beautiful vines, which are

Opposite and overleaf: *Hydrangea anomala* ssp. *petiolaris* natives of Japan, are nearly always very slow to start. They require lots of babying and seem to make little progress during their first few years. But once they decide they like the home selected for them, they will reward their keepers with lush, vigorous growth, lovely form, and long-lasting blooms.

Climbing hydrangeas can reach sixty feet (18m) in height, but forty feet (12m) is more the norm, and that's after many, many years of growth. They are frequently trained to climb walls or sturdy fences, and have also been used to cover stumps, climb trees, or even sprawl along a steep bank. The creamy white, flat, lacecap-like flowers appear in late May or early June and will often last for a month or so, unless conditions are particularly dry.

PeeGee Hydrangea

In backyards across America, massive PeeGee hydrangeas stand guard over clotheslines, vegetable gardens, old hammocks, and back porches. These are the quintessential "grandmother" shrubs, charmingly old-fashioned and endearingly lovely with long panicles that often remain on the shrub well into of bloom winter.

"PeeGee" is the shortened form of *Hydrangea paniculata* 'Grandiflora', the most common cultivar of the panicled hydrangea clan. And though beloved by generations of gardeners after its introduction from Japan in 1862, the PeeGee has been somewhat disrespected in recent years for its coarseness and a tendency to become overgrown or disheveled in maturity.

Careful pruning, however, can help the PeeGee retain a graceful shape—as a large vase, shrubby and wide, or as a tree form. And if pruned heavily to a few strong branches, this old-time favorite will produce enormous conical flowers up to eighteen inches (45cm) long and a foot (30cm) wide. The flowers begin creamy white in mid- to late summer, becoming pinkish as they age and coloring to the shade of tea-stained linen when they dry in the autumn.

Several other *Hydrangea paniculata* cultivars are grown more commonly in Europe, and are well worth an aquaintanceship:

H. paniculata *'Floribunda'*—— *A large shrub or sometimes a tree with creamy white florets that stand up on long pedicels away from the fertile flowers of the same color. The flowers take on a pink glow as they mature.*

Above: *Hydrangea paniculata* 'Pink Diamond'

42

H. paniculata 'Tardiva'—Many American growers are beginning to offer this cultivar, which is similar to 'Floribunda' but blooms later. It garnered an Award of Merit from the Royal Horticultural Society in 1966.

H. paniculata 'Pink Diamond'—Open, airy flower panicles become deep rose as they mature from their original cream color.

H. paniculata 'Praecox'— Another Award of Merit winner (1956), this early-blooming cultivar is best known for its unusual yellow-green foliage. The cream-colored flowers are like lacecaps, rather than the more typical conical shape.

Above: H. paniculata 'Tardiva' Overleaf: H. paniculata 'Grandiflora'

Wild Hydrangea

A North American native, *Hydrangea arborescens* is known by many names, including the wild hydrangea, smooth hydrangea, seven bark, bissum, and high geranium. It is also among the hardiest of all hydrangeas, with some cultivars willing to thrive in climates as chilly as Zone 3 and as warm as Zone 9.

While the species is not considered particularly noteworthy by most landscape designers, many of its cultivars are both lovely and useful in the landscape. 'Annabelle' is by far the most beloved of the *Hydrangea arborescens* group. Originating at the University of Illinois in the early part of the twentieth century, 'Annabelle' is a stunning shrub with large white flower heads blooming from mid-summer until autumn. 'Annabelle'—when grown in the lightly shaded, moist, rich conditions she prefers—will enliven any garden with her huge creamy white mopheads. An especially striking feature is the nearly chartreuse shade of the flowers when they first appear.

Another midwestern variety, 'Grandiflora' (known in some circles as 'Hills of Snow'), was found in the wild in Ohio around the turn of the century. Though not as sought after as 'Annabelle' because its big white blooms tend to droop a bit, this beautiful shrub will grow to quite massive proportions. When in full bloom, it is truly an extraordinary sight.

Opposite and overleaf: *Hydrangea arborescens* 'Annabelle'

A Few Worthy Cousins

**M**ost people are familiar with at least a few types of hydrangeas—especially the showy mophead varieties and the old-fashioned PeeGees. But even highly experienced gardeners may never have come across some of the more obscure or rare species of this large plant family. Following are a few well worth meeting.

Above: *Hydrangea villosa*   Overleaf: *H. sargentiana* and *H. aspera* 'Macrophylla'

H. involucrata 'Hortensis' —— A compact, slow-growing shrub with unusual flowers that vaguely resemble a lilac's. The tiny sepals, which appear to be layered, are pale apricot-pink with a cream or pink fertile flower. Also noteworthy are the leaves, which are large and somewhat hairy, though not prickly. The fact that this plant will grow in very alkaline soils also sets it apart.

H. sargentiana——Sargent hydrangea is a Chinese native, rarely seen in the United States, but a bit more recognized in England. In Europe it is sometimes labeled as a subspecies of Hydrangea aspera.

H. villosa——This East Asian native is sometimes cataloged as H. aspera ssp. aspera. Its delicate lacecap flowers and elongated leaves make this a special addition to the garden.

Sweet and Sour

While an extensive knowledge of the mysteries of plant science isn't essential for success in the garden, every gardener should have an understanding of what is meant by pH: it is the measure of the soil's acidity or alkalinity. Hydrangea lovers need to be aware of this important bit of scientific information because some hydrangeas—particularly the big-leaf types—have the peculiar habit of changing the color of their bloom in direct relation to the pH levels of the soil.

Put simply, in acid, or "sour," soils (those with a pH below 7.0), hydrangeas will tend to produce bluer flowers, while alkaline, or "sweet," soil (with a pH above 7.0) is more likely to create blooms in the pink to red tones. Even reliably pink varieties will tend toward blue in soil with a low pH.

To produce a more acidic soil, avoid using bone meal or superphosphates. The addition of 25-5-30 fertilizer or aluminum sulfate to the soil will also lower the pH, making the soil more acidic. For a more alkaline soil, add lime.

It should be noted that a very alkaline soil provides an unhealthy environment for most plants, including hydrangeas, because it causes interference in the plant's ability to draw nutrients from the soil.

Opposite: A range of hydrangea colors is possible, depending on the soil.

Overleaf: *H. macrophylla* in pink

The Bluest Blues

hough nature's dominant flower color is a pale pinkish mauve, blue remains the gardener's favorite hue. In the introduction to *The Color Garden (Blue)*, Bride M. Whelan writes "Blue sends an unmistakable message of calm and serenity. Sky and sea surround our world and this blueness gives comfort and assurance...the blue garden beckons and holds."

For some, the image of an intensely colored hydrangea defines the color blue. Hydrangeas, in all their variations, offer us a spectrum of blues from the silvery shimmer of the palest azure to deep, velvety, purplely hues.

And one of this extraordinary plant's greatest attributes is its ability to become even bluer. Because the acidity of the soil affects the color of the hydrangea's blooms, we can manipulate our plant's growing conditions to render the flowers in a complex palette of blues.

Gertrude Jekyll wrote in 1908 about this very type of garden trickery: "If the blue color, which comes naturally in some soils, is desired, it can be had by mixing pounded slate and iron filings with the compost—alum is another well-known agent for inducing the blue colour. But I have much faith in slate, for the bluest I have ever seen came from a garden on a slatey soil."

To improve the blue coloration of hydrangeas, today's gardener can increase the acidity of the soil by adding aluminum sulfate, which old-fashioned gardeners still call potash alum.

In the world of hydrangea aficionados, the most reliably blue cultivars are known as "good bluers," and there are a few varieties that will produce especially beautiful blue blooms even when the soil is on the sweet side. The best of the good bluers are:

Hydrangea macrophylla *'Gentian Dome'—among the bluest of all deep blues*

H. macrophylla 'Marechal Foch'——dark blue

H. macrophylla 'Generale Vicomtesse de Vibraye'——pale blue

H. serrata 'Diadem' and H. serrata 'Blue Deckle'——pale blue lacecaps

H. serrata 'Blue Billow'——intense blue; received the Pennsylvania Horticultural Society Gold Medal Award in 1990

H. macrophylla 'Blue Prince'——intensely blue mophead

H. macrophylla 'Silver Variegated Mariesii'——a lacecap with Wedgwood blue flowers when grown in acid soil; this is the variegated big-leaf variety

H. macrophylla 'Domotoi'——huge sky blue mophead that requires very acidic soil

Overleaf: *Hydrangea macrophylla* 'Generale Vicomtesse de Vibraye'

From Milky White to Cream

White flowers create a sense of peace and an aura of fantasy in an otherwise rushed and chaotic world. Deni Brown, whose beautiful book *Alba: The Book of White Flowers*, is devoted to the subject, writes, "...white is psychologically more, not less than a colour, and in most cultures has particular significance... its luminosity suggests something more spirit than flesh, an unsullied freshness and purity which signifies innocence."

White hydrangeas have elusive nuances that hint at pure snow or heavy cream, at soft clouds at midday or antique wedding dresses.

Wonderful white varieties abound, including all of the oak-leaf types, which are laden with white or creamy blooms. The big globes of wild hydrangeas, especially 'Grandiflora' and 'Annabelle', range from pure white to pale cream with a tinge of green. Many of the *Hydrangea paniculata* varieties offer creamy white flowers, too.

Among the choice white cultivars of *Hydrangea macrophylla* are:

H. macrophylla *'Lanarth White'* — *a delicate lacecap boasting pure white sepals and a surprising blue or purple center*

H. macrophylla *'Madame Emile Mouillere'* — serrated sepals
on huge, snow white mopheads that blush with pink as they age

H. macrophylla *'White Wave'* — white with a bit of pink
that changes to cream tinged with green

H. macrophylla *'Veitchii'* — white sepals with blue fertile flowers
at the center

Above: White hydrangea of unknown species   Overleaf: *H. macrophylla* 'Madame Emile Mouillere'

The Pink Palette

he pink tones of hydrangea blooms are reminiscent of cotton candy, little girls in party dresses, icy sherbet, Mother's favorite shade of lipstick, and sunrise on a summer morning. These are irresistible colors...evocative, warm, lovely to behold.

It seems that Gertrude Jekyll was quite fond of pink hydrangeas. She wrote, "...the pink flowers and fresh green foliage of the Hydrangea are also brilliant against the dusky green. It is just one simple picture that makes one glad for three months of the later summer and early autumn."

Though pink coloration can be attributed to the pH levels in the soil (a level of 6.0 to 6.5 or slightly higher will help ensure pink tones), there are some varieties of hydrangea that are reliably pink, even when soils are a bit acid. Among them are:

H. macrophylla *'Floralia'*— *pink sepals are pointed and curved*

up on their edges, giving the flowers a frilly, girlish look; beneath

the sepals, the fertile flowers range from cream to blue,

adding piquant undertones

H. paniculata *'Pink Diamond'* —— begins to flower in creamy white but slowly transform to shades of pink, until it reaches a deep rose

H. sargentiana *(Sargent's hydrangea)* —— not well known in North America but favored by European gardeners; its sterile florets are a pale, nearly white pink and the small fertile flowers contrast beautifully in deeper shades that tend toward rose

H. serrata *'Grayswood'* —— introduced in 1888 in England; has a simple lacecap flower shape, but when exposed to sunlight, the pale pink sepals of the sterile flowers darken from the ends; as the sepals mature, the margins of the sepal become a rich, deep pink

H. involucrata *'Hortensis'* —— seldom seen, but with especially delicate, dreamy apricot-pink sepals and cream and pink fertile flowers

Overleaf: *Hydrangea* 'Gertrude Glahn' (right) and *H.* 'Eldorado' (left)

Red Jewels

While pink, blue, and white hydrangeas seem to predominate in nurseries and garden centers, the reds—from deepest crimson or vermilion to softer rosy tones that are just this side of pink—have an ardent following.

Red varieties, most of them *Hydrangea macrophylla* cultivars, tend to enjoy their finest performances in a more alkaline soil, though a few are reliably red even in somewhat acidic situations.

Here, then, are a few red beauties.

H. macrophylla *'Altona'* —though the flower begins as either purplish plum or smoky blue, it becomes a vivid brick red in autumn

H. macrophylla *'Ami Pasquier'*—a crimson red

H. macrophylla *'Wesfalen'* —vivid crimson or vermilion; considered by many to be the richest red of all

H. macrophylla *'Alpengluhen'* —a German-bred cultivar; reliably produces big spheres of rosy red

H. macrophylla *'Rotschwanz'* —very deep red sepals, even in soils of 5.5 to 6.5 pH

H. macrophylla *'Brunette'* —crimson to purple; an unusual mophead that features blue centers of the sterile flower

H. serrata *'Preziosa'* —small, stunning, red to pink mopheads

Opposite: *H. serrata* 'Preziosa'   Overleaf: Unnamed cultivar of *H. macrophylla*

Perfect Garden Dwellers

Because hydrangeas on the whole are such versatile plants, there are very few limits to their use. Of course, in the coldest or warmest places, hydrangeas won't do particularly well. But in other special situations, including seaside settings, dry spots, rock gardens, or where space is limited, there are many hydrangeas that will thrive.

Few plants are able to tolerate the arduous conditions—the destructive wind, salt spray, and poor soil—of the seaside. But several hydrangeas are quite adaptable to these conditions. *Hydrangea macrophylla* 'Joseph Banks' is one of these seaside stars; according to some reports this cultivar, a mophead that blooms in shades of pale pink, white, or pale blue, even survived the devastating storms that swept the Isle of Wight in 1987, and continues to thrive.

A relative of 'Joseph Banks', *H. macrophylla* 'Lanarth White' is another hydrangea willing to live on the coast, where it will grow in full sun, a rare talent for a white hydrangea.

And *Hydrangea arborescens* 'Annabelle' and 'Grandiflora' will tolerate salt air conditions as long as they have plenty of moisture and a well-drained site.

The National Arboretum in Washington, DC, also recommends the old-fashioned PeeGee (*Hydrangea paniculata* 'Grandiflora') and oak-leaf hydrangea (*Hydrangea quercifolia*) varieties.

In the specialized configuration of a rock garden or in a pocket-sized garden, where full-sized shrubs are woefully oversized, dwarf and compact varieties are prized. Though few hydrangeas will consent to stay within such limited space, one of the smallest varieties, *Hydrangea macrophylla* 'Pia' will feel at home. She grows to a diminutive one foot (30cm) in height, but her small stature is no correlation to performance—the pink to pale red, slightly conical flower heads are enormously attractive.

Finally, for very dry places, among the most difficult of garden conditions, *H. arborescens* 'Grandiflora' is a survivor, said to tolerate even the scorching, droughty conditions found in Utah.

Above: Many hydrangeas will grow comfortably in pots.

Overleaf: *Hydrangea macrophylla* and *H. paniculata* mix beautifully in the garden.

Drying Hydrangeas

The date that the first hydrangea blossom was deliberately dried for decorative use may not be known, but the practice of preserving these exquisite blooms is certainly widespread. Hydrangea flowers are dried as huge crisp heads or as individual florets to be used in dried floral arrangements, wreaths, swags, and bouquets, and in delicate floral concoctions created petal by petal.

Hydrangeas are relatively simple to dry. It is best to pick those blooms you intend to dry at the end of the season, just before they reach their peak. As is the case with harvesting most flowers for drying, you should cut the plants on a dry day after the morning dew has evaporated.

Hydrangeas dry best when held upright in a vase that contains about two inches (5cm) of water (remove leaves first). In a few weeks the blooms will have completely dried.

Though most gardeners view dried blooms as a bit of a bonus from the garden, growing flowers for drying is actually the focus of some gardens. Because hydrangeas are among the best plants to dry, they are favorites in these specialty gardens. In fact, Stoughton House in England grows some two hundred varieties in shades of blue, white, cream, and pink.

Among the varieties of hydrangea best suited for drying are:

H. macrophylla *'Altona'* — *dries to a dark blue-green*

H. macrophylla *'Blue Wave'* — *a silvery blue when dried*

H. macrophylla *'Europa'* — *flowers dry in shades of light blue and pale green on the same heads*

H. macrophylla *'Generale Vicomtesse de Vibraye'* —sea green or dusky lilac

H. macrophylla *'Gentian Dome'* —light blue to reddish plum

H. macrophylla *'Lilacina'* —dries well with many shades of medium blue to lavender pink on each lacecap head

H. macrophylla *'Parsival'* —red-lilac to purple in sweet soil to deep blue in acid soil; the full rounded heads with large overlapping sepals have an exceptionally elegant appearance

H. macrophylla *'Madame Emile Mouillere'* —huge white mopheads that dry to a pale lime green

H. paniculata *'Unique'* —big, wide heads that dry to a pinkish beige

Above: Experiment with a variety of colors for drying.

Good Neighbors

ydrangeas make excellent companions for a host of other shrubs, perennials, bulbs, and even annuals. And gardeners continue to create new combinations, taking artistic advantage of hydrangeas' colors, whether subtle or vivid.

In order to produce a pleasing garden vignette using hydrangeas, keep in mind the forms of the dominant plants. For example, a showy mophead has a highly structured, organized shape that works well in an orderly, thoughtfully constructed composition. Thus, they look best with other well-behaved plants.

One classic and colorful composition is found throughout small towns in coastal New England. It centers on vivid blue mophead hydrangeas placed along a split rail or picket fence draped with bright pink roses. Planted among the hydrangeas are great clumps of orange daylilies. Few more beautiful sights exist!

Hydrangeas and roses do seem to enjoy each other's company. Roses in shades of seem are sighted growing alongside nearly every shade of blue hydrangea. And the red tones of varieties like *H. macrophylla* 'Alpengluhen', 'Deutschland', 'Harry's Red', or 'Wesfalen' are breathtaking with pale pink roses planted nearby.

Most daylilies, with their straplike leaves and large starry blooms, make attractive partners for hydrangeas in beds and borders. Astilbe varieties, ranging in color from red to apricot to pink to white, are wonderful planting companions for hydrangeas as well. Astilbe's delicate, feathery panicles create interesting contrasts of form and structure, and when not in bloom, the fernlike foliage stands out against the hydrangea leaf's more rounded shape.

For a pretty underplanting, hostas—especially the large-leafed ones like *Hosta sieboldiana* 'Elegans' and 'Krossa Regal'—are an excellent choice. The blue tones in their leaves are particularly effective with variegated hydrangea varieties, forming a bit of an anchor for their lighter-than-air appearance.

Above: Hydrangeas, petunias, and agapanthus keep company.

Overleaf: *H. paniculata* 'Floribunda' thrives in its woodland setting.

Prudent Cuts

ydrangeas don't tend to require a great deal of pruning, but when they do, as in the case of damage, disease, or poor appearance, the work can be a bit complicated because you must be aware of the plants' flowering patterns. Advice from Ed Broadbent, a section gardener at the prestigious Longwood Gardens in Pennsylvania, simplifies the matter for novice gardeners.

Hydrangeas bloom either on old wood (stems and branches) or on new growth. Big-leaf hydrangea (*Hydrangea macrophylla*), for example, blooms on old wood, meaning it produces buds on the branches and stems that grew in the previous growing season or earlier. These shrubs should be pruned in spring, by making cuts above strong terminal buds and removing stems that extend beyond the bud. You should also remove skimpy stems, especially those without good terminal buds, by cutting them right to the ground.

To renew a damaged or poorly shaped big-leaf hydrangea, simply cut it back to half its size, though with this treatment you will forfeit flowers that season.

PeeGee hydrangeas (*H. paniculata*) are usually pruned with a harder hand. Whether they have been trained to a single trunk form or in a multistem shape, the PeeGees should be pruned in the spring to as short as one or two buds from the ground. Many of the PeeGees may be pruned to a height of two to three and a half feet (60 to 75cm) tall. Rapid growers, they will reliably add another three feet (90cm) of growth and bloom profusely given this kind of treatment.

Like PeeGee, wild hydrangea (*Hydrangea arborescens*) blooms on current growth, so one may prune with a heavy hand in spring and still expect flowers that season.

Climbing hydrangeas and oak-leaf varieties are rarely pruned unless their shapes need a little adjusting or if a branch or stem becomes damaged. Prune damaged branches immediately. Remove awkward growth in the spring.

Above: *Hydrangea arborescens* 'Annabelle'

Overleaf: Wise cuts keep hydrangeas looking beautiful all year 'round.

Potted Hydrangeas

Around Easter and Mother's Day, florist's shops and garden centers feature pots of dwarfed pale blue hydrangeas for people to decorate tabletops with or to offer as tokens of affection. A few of these poor things will survive their arduous early upbringing, and after some tender care and nurturing may live on in a corner of the garden, though rarely as stars or even as contenders.

There are, however, many hydrangea varieties born and bred to live productive and substantial lives in containers. These special plants grace sunny patios and terraces, decks of beach houses, and balconies of city apartments.

No less a gardening light than Gertrude Jekyll herself grew hydrangeas in large terra-cotta pots at her home at Munstead Wood in Surrey. In her classic book, *Colour in the Flower Garden*, she wrote, "Now is the time to begin to use our reserve of plants in pots. Of these the most useful are the Hydrangeas. They are dropped into any vacant spaces, more or less in groups, in the two ends of the border where there is grey foliage, their pale pink colouring agreeing with these places."

A wonderful advantage of growing hydrangeas in containers is that it allows you to have complete control over the condition of the soil. Within the confines of a pot, it is a simple matter to provide the plants with rich, moist, humusy soil with just the right acidity or alkalinity in order to ensure the shade of blue or pink you adore.

Miss Jekyll's potted hydrangeas were pink mophead types. Among the many hydrangea varieties that succeed in pots are:

H. serrata *'Preziosa'* —*small mophead flowers in beautiful shades of pink and red, even in relatively acid soil*

H. serrata *'Miranda'* — a lacecap type with pale blue to white or pale pink flowers, often all colors showing at the same time

H. serrata *'Diadem'* — reliably blue to purple lacecap in nearly acidic soil, turning pink to purple when the soil is sweet

H. macrophylla *'Pia'* — a true dwarf variety, growing to only about one foot (30cm) high; the conical blooms are reliably red, fading to pink

H. macrophylla *'Merritt's Supreme'* — purplish pink mopheads that deepen as the season progresses

H. macrophylla *'Fisher's Silver Blue'* — mature flowers are slightly flattened balls of light blue or lilac with a touch of gray or silver

For those who live in less hospitable climates, growing hydrangeas in pots may be the only option, and one well worth pursuing. When the weather declines, the potted hydrangeas may be brought indoors or set in a protected place where they may reside until the temperatures climb again.

Above: A potted lacecap makes a perfect corner accent.

Overleaf: This pink mophead looks spectacular paired with a pastel geranium.

Variegata

Leaves with veins, marbling, or edges of different colors are called variegated, and they are an absolute delight in the garden, adding color, light, and the impression of movement to beds and borders. While hydrangeas are usually grown for their exquisite blooms, a variegated hydrangea is cultivated for its eye-catching foliage as well.

Hydrangea macrophylla 'Quadricolor' is one of two variegated cultivars available commercially, and is seen more often in Europe than in North America. It boasts especially vivid foliage with shades of yellow, cream, and light and dark green in irregular patterns at the margins of each leaf. 'Quadricolor' (named for those four colors present in the leaves) is a lacecap type that tends toward pale pink flowers, though it will become bluer in more acid soil. It is a small form, reaching only about four feet (1.2m) at maturity.

'Quadricolor' has a cousin, *H. macrophylla* 'Variegata Mariesii', that originated in Japan and was introduced to North American gardens in 1879. Also a lacecap type, this small shrub rarely grows to more than three feet (90cm). Its sterile marginal flowers range from nearly red to pink to light blue, depending on the acidity of the soil. Each leaf of 'Variegata Mariesii' is edged in ivory, with some leaves more heavily variegated than others.

Another variegated example is *H. macrophylla* 'Maculata'; though a pretty plant with white and light green markings on the leaf edges, it is not well known to North American gardeners.

Variegated hydrangeas seem to be a bit more tender than other types, and will sometimes suffer from short-term frost damage. Once the dead branches are pruned away, the shrub will rebound happily, though if there is extensive damage, flowering may be compromised.

Opposite: *Hydrangea macrophylla* 'Quadricolor'
Overleaf: Delicately mottled petals add to the hydrangea's variable beauty.

Year-Round Beauty

 hough hydrangeas bring to mind visions of sumptuous flowers in lush colors, those who live with them understand and appreciate their ability to add beauty to the landscape all year long.

In autumn, as the oak-leaf hydrangea's blooms pale and dry to a crisp, the leaves darken and color until they are vivid in tones of red, burgundy, and deep maroon. But the oak-leaf hydrangea is only one of many family members with talents that reveal themselves beyond the season of bloom.

For especially beautiful autumn foliage color, *Hydrangea serrata* 'Preziosa' turns to exquisite, nearly shimmering bronze tones after a frost. *Hydrangea paniculata* 'Praecox' is another plant prized for autumn foliage—this one sparkles in an intense gold-yellow.

Several members of the *Hydrangea macrophylla* clan are cool-weather charmers. *H. macrophylla* 'Grant's Choice' boasts rich coppery foliage, while *H. macrophylla* 'Tokyo Delight' has leaves of russet red that become nearly purple as the autumn progresses.

H. macrophylla 'Nigra' leaves turn a rich bronze in autumn, and the variety sports unusual black or dark purple stems. And it is difficult to find a more breathtaking sight than a perfect hydrangea bloom encased in frost.

Opposite: Vibrant red hydrangea leaves decorate the autumn landscape.

Overleaf: Hydrangea blooms are crystallized with frost.

Accenting Garden Structures and Trees

**B**illowing hydrangea shrubs are ideal for softening the sometimes harsh lines of garden walls and outbuildings. The shrubs are substantial enough to have a true impact, yet airy enough to provide soothing contrast to the solidity of brick or stone or stucco. Flower colors from subtle pastels to vibrant hues complement stone or weathered shingles, particularly.

The quite rugged climbing hydrangeas are also perfect partners to garden walls. Though slow to get established, they'll eventually wend their way along a wall (if given adequate support), offering a generous cascade of snowy white blooms.

Training a climbing hydrangea to clamber up the trunk of a tree is a design device few gardeners attempt, though it is no more difficult than training one on a fence or a wall. The tree should be limbed high and must have some texture to the bark. Honey locusts, tulip poplars, shagbark hickory, white pine, and spruce make hospitable hosts to the climbing hydrangea.

To achieve the most beautiful effect for a tree-climbing hydrangea, select a woodland setting, where the hydrangea's huge white flower heads will illuminate shady patches of green, gray, and brown tones. Climbing hydrangeas tend to have a slightly wild appearance, especially when they become old and gnarled.

Opposite: A lacecap ornaments an iron gate.   Overleaf: Climbing hydrangea scrambles over a garden wall.

Natural Plantings

hile hydrangeas have long been used in country flower gardens and city plots alike, many gardeners overlook the possibilities of using them in wild settings or woodland gardens. On the dappled edges of clearings, mixed with ferns and other forest natives, many hydrangeas are perfectly at home. Make sure to choose a species or cultivar that will tolerate some shade, and select a color that will blend harmoniously with the rest of the landscape.

Consider particularly *Hydrangea arborescens*—commonly called wild hydrangea, seven bark, or high geranium—which originated in the Appalachian Mountains. Its cousin, *Hydrangea quercifolia*, known as the oak-leaf hydrangea for its distinctive leaf form, is also a worthy addition to a woodland garden or other natural landscape. These two species, discovered only relatively recently, retain a wilder, less lush appearance than their oft-hybridized relatives. Garden-worthy varieties of both the oak-leaf and the wild hydrangea have been bred by nurserymen, and are widely available. Be sure to give thought to the descendants of these two wild shrubs when plotting your natural landscape.

Opposite: Hydrangeas brighten a woodland garden.

On Display

In public and private gardens throughout the world, hydrangeas are cast in both leading and supporting roles. In some places, the hydrangeas shamelessly steal the summer scene, while in other gardens, they shy away from the limelight, preferring instead to add subtle delights along a path or in a border.

Outside Philadelphia, at the Morris Arboretum, there is a large collection of many types and varieties of hydrangeas including native oak-leafs and wild examples. Of particular note is the unusual black-stem big-leaf variety (*H. macrophylla* 'Nigra') and the shaggy hydrangea (*H. heteromalla* 'Bretschneideri').

Also in Pennsylvania, at the renowned Longwood Gardens in Kennett Square, there is a large and varied collection of hydrangeas, with a special emphasis on oak-leaf varieties in the native plant area.

Any serious pilgrimage to see the world's best hydrangeas should include a visit to Holehird Gardens in Windermere, Cumbria, in England. Owned by the Lakeland Horticultural Society, Holehird is the home of England's National Collection of hydrangeas. Among those on display are H. *arborescens* 'Annabelle', H. *anomala* ssp. *petiolaris*, and dozens of cultivars of H. *macrophylla*.

A newly created assemblage of hydrangeas, said to be the largest in the world, with more than 600 plants on display, is the Shamrock Hydrangea Collection at Varengeville-sur-Mer in Normandy, France. Included are *H. macrophylla* varieties such as 'Mariesii', 'Zeisig', 'Jogasaki', and 'Rosea'.

At Tintinhull House in Somerset, a garden made famous by Penelope Hobhouse, hydrangeas are grouped in the Middle Garden which, though confined within high walls, retains a woodland atmosphere. Here you can see the *Hydrangea aspera* 'Villosa' that was found by legendary plant collector E.H. Wilson on one of his many expeditions to Asia in the early 1900s. In Tintinhull's sweet soil the shrub blooms pink, though it tends to be a lilac-blue where the soil is more acidic.

At Kiftsgate Court, a private garden open to the public outside Chipping Campden in Gloucestershire, there are groups of *Hydrangea aspera* 'Villosa' reaching up to 15 feet (4.5m) tall.

One of England's favorite garden writers, Christopher Lloyd, uses masses of *Hydrangea arborescens* 'Annabelle' in the long mixed border at Great Dixter, his home in Sussex, which is open to the public on a regular schedule. The plants' large, creamy flower heads, with their undertones of pale green, make truly dramatic highlights.

Other gardens with notable hydrangea displays include:

The Arnold Arboretum
Jamaica Plain, Massachusettes

Arboretum of the Barnes
    Foundation
Merion Station, Pennsylvania

Callaway Gardens
Pine Mountain, Georgia

University of Washington
    Arboretum
Seattle, Washington

New York Botanical Gardens
Bronx, New York

Royal Botanic Gardens at Kew
Richmond, Surrey
England

Winterthur Museum and
    Gardens
Winterthur, Delaware

Vancouver Botanic Gardens
Vancouver, British Columbia,
Canada

Royal Horticulture Gardens,
    Wisley
Woking, Surrey
England

Borde Hill Garden
Haywards Heath, West Sussex,
England

Strybing Arboretum and
    Botanical Gardens
San Francisco, California

U.S. National Arboretum
Washington, DC

Munchen Botanischer Garten
Munich, Germany

Chicago Botanic Garden
Glencoe, Illinois

Hidcote Manor Gardens
Chipping Campden,
Gloucestershire
England

John F. Kennedy Arboretum
County Wexford
Ireland

Secrest Arboretum
Wooster, Ohio
Garden in the Woods
Framingham, Massachusettes

Cheekwood Botanical Gardens
Nashville, Tennessee

Filoli Center
Woodside, California

Le Parc Floral des Moutiers
Varengeville-sur-Mer,
Normandy, France

Stourton House
Stourton, Wiltshire
England

Tresco Abbey
Isles of Scilly, Cornwall,
England

Melbourne Botanic Gardens
Melbourne
Australia

For Further Reading

Hydrangeas—A Gardener' Guide by Toni Lawson-Hall and Brian Rothera. Portland, OR: Timber Press, 1995.

This is the definitive work on the genus *Hydrangea* by the experts responsible for building the National Collection of Hydrangeas at Windermere in England.

Hydrangeas by Corinne Mallet. Paris, France: Centre d'Art Floral, 1994.

A reference book by a French expert who operates the Shamrock Hydrangea Collection in Normandy. Call 35-85-17-13 to obtain a copy.

Plants That Merit Attention: Volume II—Shrubs by Janet Meakin Poor and Nancy Peterson Brewster. Portland, OR: Timber Press and The Garden Club of America, 1996.

Brief, but useful descriptions of wild, oak-leaf, French, and PeeGee hydrangeas include substantial information about each plant's landscape value.

Flowering Shrubs and Small Trees by Isabel Zucker. New York, NY: Friedman/Fairfax, 1995.

An enclopedic approach to the subject with lists of flowering shrubs for every purpose.

The Gardener's Guide to Britain by Patrick Taylor. Portland, OR: Timber Press, 1997.

An essential guide to hundreds of gardens, nurseries, and garden centers open to the public in England, Scotland, and Wales.

On Gardening by Penelope Hobhouse. New York, NY: Macmillan, 1994.

One of gardening's greatest devotes a short chapter to hydrangeas in this beautiful and inspirational book.

Rosemary Verey's Garden Plans by Rosemary Verey. London, England: Frances Lincoln Publishers, 1993.

Photos and plot plans for several different styles of gardens.

American Mixed Border by Ann Lovejoy. New York, NY: Macmillan, 1993.

Good ideas for seamless blending of trees, shrubs, perennials, grasses, and bulbs.

Best Borders by Tony Lord. New York, NY: Viking, 1993.

Invaluable resource for creating mixed border of shrubs, perennials, bulbs, and other plants.

The Border Book by Anna Pavord. New York, NY: Dorling Kindersley, 1994.
Drawings of garden plans with useful descriptions of the plants.

Variegated Leaves—The Encyclopedia of Patterned Foliage by Susan Conder. New York, NY: Macmillan Publishing, 1993.

How to grow and use variegated plants, including hydrangeas.

The Color Garden (Blue), (White) by Elvin McDonald. San Francisco, CA: Collins Publishers, 1995.

A pretty series on monochromatic gardens.

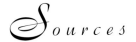

Sources

Hydrangeas, because they are so universally beloved, are almost always available at nurseries and garden centers. However, many are sold as generic "pink" or "blue" flowering shrubs. For those whose interest runs a bit deeper, it is worth the effort to seek out knowledgeable and reliable sources in order to obtain specific varieties and cultivars.

The following list of nurseries, growers, and plant breeders, with a partial listing of what they offer, is a place to start. When interest develops into passion, these sources will likely produce further information.

Bressingham Gardens
Bressingham, Diss
Norfolk IP22 2AB
England
Tel: 01379 687386.
  H. arborescens 'Annabelle,' *H. macrophylla* ssp. *serrata* 'Preziosa,' *H. paniculata* 'Tardiva,' *H. quercifolia* 'Snowflake'

Carroll Gardens
444 E. Main St.
Westminster, MD 21157
(800) 638-6334
  H. paniculata, H. aborescens

Fairweather Gardens
P.O. Box 330
Greenwich, NJ 08323
H. paniculata 'Tardiva'

Gossler Farms
1200 Weaver Road
Springfield, OR 97478
(541) 746-3922
  Wide assortment of varieties.

Heronswood Nursery
7530 288th St. NE
Kingston, WA 98346
  Many varieties, some difficult to find, of *H. arborescens, H. macrophylla,* and *H. paniculata*

Hillier's Nurseries Ltd.
Ampfield House, Ampfield
Hampshire SO51 9PA
England
Tel: 01794 368733
  H. arborescens 'Annabelle,' *H. macrophylla* 'White Wave,' *H. paniculata*. 'Tardiva'

Hydrangeas Plus
P.O. Box 389
Aurora, OR 97002
  Many varieties of H. marcro phylla, H. arborescens, and H. paniculata

Imperatore Nurseries
Windy Bush Road
New Hope, PA 18938
(2115) 598-7882
  Many varieties sold to the trade.

Louisiana Nursery
Opelousas, LA
(318) 948-3696
  H. aspera, H. quercifolia

Roslyn Nursery
211 Burns Lane
Dix Hills, NY 11746
  H. quercifolia 'Snowflake,' *H. paniculata* 'Tardiva'

Shamrock Hydrangea Collection
766229 Varengeville-sur-Mer
Normandy, France
35-85-10-02
  Many varieties sold to the trade.

SOURCES (CONTINUED)

Wayside Gardens
Hodges, South Carolina
(800) 845-1124
   H. arborescens 'Annabelle,' *H.
paniculata* 'Grandiflora,' *H.
petiolaris, H. paniculata*
'Tardiva,' *H. macrophylla*
'Forever Pink, *H. macrophylla*
'Pia,' *H. macrophylla* 'Blue
Wave,' *H. macrophylla* 'Nikko
Blue.'

White Flower Farm
P.O. Box 50
Litchfield, Connecticut 06759
(800) 503 9624
   H. petiolaris, H. paniculata
'Tardiva', *H. arborescens*
'Annabelle', *H. macrophylla* 'Blue
Billow', *H. m.* 'Variegata
Maresii', *H. serrata* 'Preziosa'

$\mathcal{O}$*rganizations*

American Hydrangea Society
P.O. Box 11645
Atlanta, GA
   Publishes a quality newsletter

Friends of the Shamrock
Hydrangea Collection
Route de l'Eglise
76119 Varengeville Sur Mer
France
   Publishes a newsletter about
the development of the collection

PHOTOGRAPHY

Front jacket and flap photography:
©Steve Terrill
Back jacket photography: ©Steve
Terrill

©Charles Crust: p. 96

©Carolyn Fox: pp. 14, 31

The Garden Picture Library: ©Rex
Butcher: p. 7; ©Sunniva Harte: pp. 28,
34 background and top, 36-37, 101;
©Juliette Wade: p. 29; ©Didier
Willery: pp. 38, 72-73; ©Steven
Wooster: pp. 40-41, 89 foreground;
©David Russell: p. 50 bottom; ©Neil
Holmes: pp. 66, 68-69, 74, 80, 84;
©Mayer/Le Scanff: pp. 75, 94-95;
©Andrea Jones: pp. 1, 104; ©Christian
Williams: p. 105

©John Glover: pp. 17 foreground, 21
foreground, 32-33, 42 foreground, 48-
49, 70, 71, 76-77, 78, 79 all, 88, 89
background, 102-103
©Michael Habicht: p. 12

©Bill Johnson: pp. 30, 43 foreground, 47

©Andrea Jones: Garden Design by
Maurice Foster of Ivy Hatch near
Sevenoaks, Kent: pp. 8, 19, 25, 52-53,
60-61, 63, 93, Courtesy of Lost
Gardens of Heligan, Cornwall: pp. 9,
13

©Dency Kane: pp. 24, 85

©Kenneth E. Meyer: pp. 16 background, 17 background, 26-27, 35

©Clive Nichols: pp. 56-57, 62, 64-65,
90-91; Garden Design by Chenies
Manor, Bucks: p. 81; Garden Design
by RHS Garden, Wisley: pp. 82-83;
Garden Design by Lakemount, Cork,
Eire: pp. 86-87

©Jerry Pavia: pp. 34 bottom, 42 background, 43 background, 44-45

Positive Images: ©Jerry Howard: p. 39

©Steve Terrill: pp.1, 2-3 all, 6, 10, 11,
16 foreground, 18, 22-23, 50 top, 54,
58 - 59 all, 97, 98-99, 100